Go Make
DISCIPLES

Embracing **PEOPLE AFFECTED** by **DISABILITY** Through **MENTORING RELATIONSHIPS**

Mike Dobes

 THE IRRESISTIBLE CHURCH SERIES

Copyright © 2018 Joni and Friends

Go Make Disciples
Print: ISBN 978-1-946237-20-0
Kindle: ISBN 978-1-946237-21-7
EPUB: ISBN 978-1-946237-22-4

Author: Mike Dobes
Collaborators: Bruce Zachary, Cate Given
Contributing Editor: Ali Howard
Editor in Chief: Eric Jones

All rights reserved. No part of this book may be used
or reproduced in any manner whatsoever without the
written permission of the publisher.

Printed in the United States of America.

Scripture quotations are taken from the
Holy Bible, *English Standard Version*®, ESV®, copyright © 2001
by Crossway Bibles, a publishing ministry of Good News Publishers.
Used by permission. All rights reserved.

Produced by The Denzel Agency (www.denzel.org)
Cover and Interior Design: Rob Williams

For information, rights and permissions, or to order additional print
copies of this and other resources, contact the publisher:

Joni and Friends International Disability Center
P.O. Box 3333, Agoura Hills, California 91376-3333
Email: churchrelations@joniandfriends.org
Phone: 818-707-5664

Kindle version available at www.irresistiblechurch.org

CONTENTS

Why Another Book on Leadership?

Leadership is a topic that has been addressed over and over. It is the subject of countless books, blogs, sermons, podcasts, and conferences. So why did we feel the need to write about this topic again? Our hope is to combine the concepts of leadership and disability ministry in a unique way with the goal of helping churches become more irresistible. *An Irresistible Church is an authentic community built on the hope of Christ that compels people affected by disability to fully belong.* It takes a unique style and heart of leadership to truly care for and advocate on behalf of individuals affected by disability. In addition to this, irresistible leadership is not merely about leading individuals affected by disability. Rather, it is about creating space for everybody who is called into leadership to come, grow, and express their gifts and talents. Healthy leadership does not happen *to* people affected by disability, nor does it only happen *for* them. It should happen *with* them. Ideally, they should be part of the leadership pipeline, contributing and fully belonging according to the calling God has placed on their lives. As an irresistible leader, it is essential to not see people affected by disability as objects of leadership, but rather as participants in leadership. Irresistible leadership strives to design and maintain the authentic community that many families and individuals seek.

A typical approach to leadership simply does not address all the nuances of disability ministry. A distinct perspective and an open heart are needed to fully include and celebrate people affected by disability within circles of leadership. God is looking for people who will follow the example of Christ in action and in attitude. In contrast to the religious leaders of his day, Jesus did not see people affected by disability as hindrances to ministry, but as individuals created in the image of God. *God is looking for leaders to not only serve people affected by disability, but also to mentor and disciple them into places of influence.* If this book was given to you, it is probably because somebody else sees you as this kind of leader. If you picked this book up on your own, perhaps the Holy Spirit is prompting you to embrace a fresh style of leadership that you never thought possible. Regardless of the reason, thank you! Thank you for having an open heart, and together, let's become irresistible leaders who lead churches and ministries where people affected by disability may fully belong!

In exploring the concept of irresistible leadership, the following chapters will guide our steps and help us lead in a way that makes space for the entire body of Christ to participate. The first step toward leadership is to *consider the necessity of surrendering to God* and remaining in constant conversation and submission to his guidance in our lives. In its simplest form, this involves our relationship with God and our relationship with others. Next, we must *consider the idea of calling*. Who are you? Who has God created you to be? How can you lead with excellence in your area of calling? After considering these important concepts, it is essential to *define what irresistible leadership is and how it functions*. Then, we will look at a four-step roadmap to *identify, equip, and release new leaders* that will allow for greater impact and influence of your leadership. Finally, we will examine *the results of irresistible leadership* and the difference this leadership model can make in your life, in your church or ministry, and in your community.

As you continue reading this book, please pause for a moment and ask the Holy Spirit to soften your heart and help you grow. There may be new ideas that stretch you and help you discover different ways of seeing God's people. I encourage you to be open to this. As a pastor walking this same road with you, I can confidently say that it is well worth any passing moments of discomfort and misunderstanding to gain a deeper understanding of loving and leading God's people.

Surrendering to God

While our calling can be fluid through different seasons of life, there is one over-arching quality that should define every effective leader: a vibrant relationship with Jesus Christ. Our personal walk with God directly influences our ability to lead others; it is only through his strength and grace that we have anything sustainable to offer to others.

While many of us already know this, allow me a quick moment to encourage you. Our personal walk with the Lord typically includes the following components: Bible reading, journaling and meditating on the Word, worship, prayer, serving, and corporate gatherings. It is easy to view these practices as checkboxes completed on a weekly basis rather than as tools or ways by which we keep our relationship with God fresh and vibrant. Too often, the demands and expectations of daily life cause us to compromise our personal relationship with God. When we struggle with feeling tired and rundown, it might be that we are not resting in the Lord like he desires us to. Slow down, run to the feet of Jesus, and do what you must to remain there. As somebody who has spent far too many years in ministry running on my own strength, trust me when I say, it is worth slowing down. As many wise leaders have said, we can only lead people as far as we ourselves have gone. There is no area of leadership that holds more importance than the personal walk we are privileged to have with God. It is only out of our relationship with God that we can have healthy relationships with others.

Your Relationship with God

The true measure of success in every area of life comes down to our relationship with God. We can be busy with many good things, but outside of his presence we will never truly experience the relationship and abundance he has in store for us. We must fight against becoming so busy with life, work, and ministry that we do not spend time in the sacred space where God meets us. Throughout the Bible, we see that different leaders met with God in diverse ways, but they all had a sacred space where they came before the Lord. David met God in the pasture with his sheep, while Moses was visited by God in the desert.

Even Jesus went away to isolated places to reconnect and recharge with his Father.

Where is your sacred space? Where can you quiet your mind to focus on Christ and sense his presence in a unique and personal way? For me, it is at the beach during sunset. The sound of crashing waves, the magnificent colors, and the expanse of ocean not only remind me just how small I am, but the beach affords me the environment to know and be known by God. Maybe you prefer pine trees on a mountaintop, your favorite chair by a fireplace, or even a local coffee shop. The location doesn't matter nearly as much as the discipline to spend time quieting your heart before the Lord on a regular basis.

Psalm 37:7a encourages us to "be still before the Lord and wait patiently for him." Psalm 46:10a also tells us that knowing God happens when we are still. Stillness, quiet, waiting, solitude—these are not words that most people would use to describe me. I am definitely a type-A, loud, fill-the-room-and-be-the-life-of-the-party kind of guy. Yet, my soul withers quickly and my spirit can become parched when I do not make space in my life for the still, small voice of God.

These verses are about *being*, not *doing*. God is not instructing us to "do stillness" but rather simply to be. This is not a task to accomplish, a tower to build, a checkbox to tick. This is so much deeper. It is a soulful, Spirit-led activity that fills the chambers of my inner man and drowns out the noise and activity of the world around me. I must remember that God first asks me to *be* before he asks me to *do*. I am his child because of relationship, not accomplishment. I encourage you today to rest in the thought that God created you as a unique and beloved human being.

As leaders, we must make intentional plans to spend time in our sacred space—just as we would any other important activity in life. Many of us start our mornings with a (very necessary) cup of coffee and some devotions. However, our stillness and sacred space cannot stop there. God designed us for Sabbath. This rhythm of life is important and should not be ignored. Sometimes, the only way to have sacred space is to say no to other things. I know, I know—it seems very un-Christian to not be available for every good opportunity to serve, lead, attend, or minister. In Western Christianity, we have been conditioned to believe that true servants of God are busy. I used to embody this belief, but I struggled to find biblical support for this concept. Instead, as I studied Scripture, I saw that God calls us to a daily rhythm in his presence—a dance if you will. The only way that I can lead effectively is to say no to good opportunities that may threaten my daily rhythm.

What might this daily rhythm look like?

> *Psalm 5:3*—"O Lord, in the morning you hear my voice; in the morning I prepare a sacrifice for you and watch."

> *Psalm 23*—This psalm shows us that God guides our every step; it is he who leads us to rest, through danger, and into seasons of peace and righteousness.

> *Psalm 55:16-17*—"But I call to God, and the Lord will save me. Evening and morning and at noon I utter my complaint and moan, and he hears my voice."

> *Daniel 6:10*—"[Daniel] got down on his knees three times a day and prayed and gave thanks before his God, as he had done previously."

Mark 1:35—"And rising very early in the morning, while it was still dark, he [Jesus] departed and went out to a desolate place, and there he prayed."

Acts 16:25—"About midnight Paul and Silas were praying and singing hymns to God."

Psalm 63:1—"O God, you are my God; earnestly I seek you; my soul thirsts for you; my flesh faints for you, as in a dry and weary land where there is no water."

There is no perfect formula for seeking God. The key is to give him your best time and your best energy. We are to earnestly pursue God daily. Perhaps you are a morning person or maybe you are more of an evening person. The key is to build a rhythm that works for you and allows you to spend time daily in the Word of God, in conversation with God, listening to God, and then, after all that, serving God. I encourage you to find and fiercely protect your sacred space. Doing so will strengthen your relationship with God and influence your relationship with others.

Your Relationship with Others

When the Pharisees asked Jesus which of the commandments given to the Israelites was the greatest, he identified two. First, "love the Lord your God with all your heart and with all your soul and with all your mind" (Matthew 22:37). But then he added a second command to this one: we are to love our neighbor as we love ourselves. Our neighbors are not geographically bound to the homes next door or across the street, though it certainly includes them. Our neighbor is anyone who crosses our path as we go about our daily business. In his response, Jesus highlighted the importance of both loving God and loving others. It is impossible to be a leader in the kingdom of God if we are unable to see value in everybody around us. We must see the world through the eyes of God, and we must be willing to serve others in humility and grace.

There was a running joke within the staff at one church where I was employed: ministry would be so much easier if it wasn't for all the people. Truth be told, this joke was part of how we helped one another process the struggles and challenges that come with leadership. Over the years, God has slowly changed my perspective. Instead of worrying about who people are, I am now more focused on how I see them. This shift, although slight, completely alters how I interact with, pray for, influence, and lead the people in my life. It puts the responsibility for the relationship on me, and it reduces the opportunities for me to blame others when plans go awry.

So, what does your relationship with others look like? If we are not careful, it is very possible to see people as a means to an end. If we have a project to complete or a task to accomplish, then we need people around to assist us. With this perspective, we are tempted to see people simply as tools for our benefit and, when the project is done, the need for those people comes to an end. Unfortunately, I must confess that in my early years of ministry, this perspective dominated my thinking. While I rarely voiced the idea, I often valued people based on the skills they had and how that would benefit me. Caring for them as a person and fostering their journey with God definitely took a backseat. Thankfully, by the grace of God, this perspective is no longer a regular temptation for me.

Perhaps you see people as partners in ministry. We can work side by side and be aware of the larger context of life that extends far beyond any project or task on which we might be working. This is a far healthier perspective as it gives value to others beyond their skills. While it is important to work hard and to do things with excellence, it is more important to ask what God is doing in the lives of others and if there is anything we can do to assist them in their journey with him. Authority is passed on, innovation is celebrated, and people join a project or cause, not merely because of what they can do, but because they feel that they can contribute in a valuable and personal way. The shortcoming of this perspective is that people are still seen for what they can contribute. It limits the scope of relational influence to those who might contribute on a practical level.

What if we were able to simply see people as beloved sons or daughters created in the image of God? What if my primary and motivating concern was pointing others to Christ? What if the accomplishment of tasks and projects, while important, was not the motivating factor for engaging in relationship? This would open the door to countless opportunities to share the gospel with others. Admittedly, it is challenging to battle my selfish nature that consistently rises up and screams, "What's in it for me?!", but this is the very battle in which an irresistible leader must engage.

Effective ministry is generally accomplished through relationships. The very nature of ministry involves people. A key factor of irresistible leadership is to connect people with common passions and complementary gifts who have a humble desire to serve rather than be served. Effective ministry makes room for people affected by disability, for people with wonderful ministry experience, for people with no experience, and for people whom only God would choose to lead. Please keep healthy relationships as a higher priority over skills, education, and experience.

I want to see people through the eyes of God and love them the way that he loves me. I don't believe that his primary motive in loving me is because of the amazing skills that I have. He loves me simply because of who I am. It's not about what I produce or the talents with which I have been blessed. It is from *this* perspective and framework of life that effective leadership, and, thereby, ministry, might occur.

Identifying Your Calling

Leadership is personal. It involves relationships and sacrifice. Leadership involves risk-taking, vision, and caring for others. Truthfully, leadership is a big task that can only be accomplished in partnership with God. When we answer God's call to leadership, we are enlisting for a life of giving ourselves away for the benefit of others. This is not a calling that should be taken lightly. Rather, leaders have the potential to transform communities, impact churches and ministries, and influence others for eternity. As leaders, this is what we are called to! Leaders typically share a common story that involves feeling "called" by God into their role or place of service. Yet, many of us cannot clearly share what this calling looks like, feels like, or how it might effectively direct our steps.

We spend a great deal of time in the ministry world talking about our calling. But how do we know if we are called to leadership? While this is an important concept, what does it actually mean? I felt called to children's ministry out of Bible college. My calling then shifted to youth ministry, then to teaching ministry, and currently to disability ministry. Did God keep changing his mind about my career? Was I terrible at my previous ministry positions and have only now found a position that fits my strengths?

I have worked with countless people over the years who are desperately seeking God's calling for their lives. The particulars of our calling will vary during different seasons in each of our lives. Family might be your primary calling for a time, after which you might transition into serving at your church or a local ministry or even a community organization. Ultimately, there is only one calling: to live a life that brings glory to God. This might happen through sports, writing, parenting, or vocational ministry. What matters, according to Colossians 3:17, is that we do everything for the glory of God.

However, we are each called to specific spheres of influence, and no, I do not believe that God changes his mind concerning our influence. Rather, our calling is flexible according to several factors. Over my years in ministry, I have identified three factors that have acted as a wonderful filter through which I determine where I should serve. These include our skills, our passions, and the opportunities presented to us. Allow me to elaborate on this filtering system.

Skills—I feel that within the Christian community, we often overlook the importance of skills by saying that if we are called to serve we shouldn't be hindered by whether we are the best fit. This may be true when it comes to meeting an immediate need, but I can tell you that you do not want me serving as a long-term counselor, the overseer of the benevolence fund, or many other church ministries that I simply do not have the skill set for. Are you comfortable with your skill set and confident in who God made you to be? Do you recognize that being affected by disability does not exclude anybody from leadership, as we all have skills in various areas? We need to serve with excellence (not perfection), and God has provided each of us with areas where we are a 10. Identifying those areas is a wonderful way to start determining our calling.

Passion—Passion is an essential component of your calling. God will not ask us to serve long-term in a position that drains the life from us. That would be detrimental not only to ourselves but also to those we are serving. Yes, there are seasons of serving outside our passion to meet a need, but ministry calling should fire you up and fuel your passion, not suck the life out of you. What keeps you up at night? What do you hear on the news or from friends that deeply moves your heart? Do you have a passion to serve and minister alongside people affected by disability? What would you do every day even if you were never paid for it? Ask yourself these questions to help identify your passion.

Opportunity—It is extremely difficult to engage in your calling if there are no open doors to walk through. When I transitioned from children's ministry to youth ministry, it was not because I was tired of children's ministry. Rather, a door opened for youth ministry, and as I prayed and considered the opportunity, my excitement and passion grew. Be encouraged that your time might be better spent seeking the open doors God has already placed in your life instead of attempting to knock down the locked door beside you. Do you feel that disability might close the door to opportunity, for yourself personally or for others, or are you able to creatively adapt? What if an opportunity or need presents itself, but you don't feel particularly skilled in or passionate about the opportunity?

With these three factors in mind, I encourage you to create some sort of chart🐢 that highlights your

---

🐢 This symbol indicates that there are supplemental resources that correspond with this topic at http://irresistiblechurch.org/library/

skills, your passions, and the opportunities before you. I would also suggest that you enlist trusted family members, friends, and ministry leaders to share about the gifts they see in you. Then, after prayer, don't be afraid to jump in, serve well, and allow God to shape your calling in the midst of your work. He is faithful, he has plans and dreams for you, and he will call you to a position where your skills, your passions, and your opportunities come together in perfect harmony.

Defining Irresistible Leadership

Leadership is influence. As a leader, your church or ministry will reflect your heart, your passion, and your values. Effective leadership has very little to do with a formal title or role. Before you can consider leading an *Irresistible Church*, it is essential to determine if you, personally, are an irresistible leader. But what exactly does this mean?

In Ephesians 3, Paul addresses the heart of God and the grace extended to Gentiles. People who were once excluded from the family of God are now invited to fully belong and partake of the blessings of heaven. There is equal belonging, equal blessing, equal participation in the body of Christ. This is a great mystery of God, yet it is a beautiful picture of what heaven will look like as everybody, whether they have great success or have been marginalized and cast aside, is united in worship. Gentiles had to be pursued and brought into fellowship with Jews, and in the same way, families affected by disability often have to be pursued and brought into fellowship with the Church. There has been too much hurt, too much neglect, and too much ignoring. An irresistible leader confidently raises a banner of justice, pursues a culture of belonging, and tirelessly serves families affected by disability. The result? The body of Christ is made whole, those who once were lost are now found, and the marginalized and outcast of society find a family where they are loved, cherished, and celebrated!

As I mentioned earlier, an *Irresistible Church is an authentic community built on the hope of Christ that compels people affected by disability to fully belong.* In the following pages, you will find a handful of questions related to this definition that I regularly ask myself. I hope they will be helpful to you as you consider how you can become an irresistible leader. The greatest leaders typically discover areas for improvement both through internal assessment and by receiving external input. May this quick assessment help you develop as a leader through both paths. I would encourage you to not only answer these questions individually, but to ask a few trusted people in your inner circle to answer them about you as well.

An authentic community—How can a leader develop and maintain an authentic community? Are you transparent and vulnerable? Not to everybody you meet, but to those who are close to you? Do they know your dreams and fears? Do they know your struggles and victories? Do people feel safe to be real with you, knowing that you love them regardless? What does community look like for you—are you living in a vacuum or is fellowship an essential piece of your life?

Built on the hope of Christ—When everything around you is in turmoil, where do you turn? If you turn to your leadership skills, your bank account, or even your friends, I am concerned that more turmoil is coming your way because ultimately all these things will eventually fail. Are you personally built on the hope of Christ? Is Christ the center of your life? Is he your rock and salvation, your strength and peace, your hope? Is your life built on him in such a way that the greatest storms of life might howl and even cause the world around you to shudder and fall, but you remain standing because your foundation is untouchable?

That compels people affected by disability—When you are outside the context of ministry, how do you interact with people affected by disability? Do you have friends with disabilities in your everyday life, or are they only objects of ministry and compassion? Are you willing to recognize the disabilities in others and embrace them as leaders? Do you find yourself annoyed because somebody is moving slower, or do you reach out and ask if you might assist them in any way? Are you able to recognize your own disabilities? Our society today tends to be very self-focused, and we must ask God to transform our hearts in such a way that people are drawn into relationship with us because they sense we genuinely care. They ought to be attracted to the peace and presence of God in our lives.

To fully belong—Belonging is something that we all desire. We want to know that we are loved and cared for. We want to know that we are missed when we are absent. We want a chance to share our gifts, to serve others, and to be valuable. Again, are people affected by disability welcome in your everyday life, or only in your ministry? Are you able to see people for their abilities before you see their disabilities? Do you see the leadership calling and abilities that are just as prevalent in your friends affected by disability as within yourself?

An irresistible leader is one who oversees an authentic community built on the hope of Christ that compels people affected by disability to fully belong.

The culture and environment of your church will be a direct reflection of you. Do you lead with compassion or impatience? Are you known for listening well or blindly giving directions? What happens when an individual desires to attend your church and does not seem to fit into the program? God is calling us as leaders to be more about relationship than activity. Servant leadership cannot simply be a slick marketing phrase, a well-designed T-shirt, or a poster on the wall. We must live out Philippians 2 and look not only to our own interests, our own tasks, our own leadership challenges, but also to the interests of others.

Roadmap for Leadership

While every experience differs and each of us has a unique route to leadership depending upon our personal story, gifts, and calling, there are certain principles of leadership development that are universal. In the Old Testament, Moses' father-in-law, Jethro, provides a practical four-step roadmap📚 in his leadership challenge to Moses:

> Now obey my voice; I will give you advice, and God be with you! You shall represent the people before God and bring their cases to God, and you shall warn them about the statutes and the laws, and make them know the way in which they must walk and what they must do. Moreover, look for able men from all the people, men who fear God, who are trustworthy and hate a bribe, and place such men over the people as chiefs of thousands, of hundreds, of fifties, and of tens. And let them judge the people at all times. Every great matter they shall bring to you, but any small

matter they shall decide themselves. So, it will be easier for you, and they will bear the burden with you. (Exodus 18:19-22)

In this passage we see Jethro encourage Moses to model leadership, identify potential leaders, coach them, and release them into ministry. The reason that leadership development is crucial for your ministry is that doing ministry by yourself is simply not scalable. Developing leaders allows you to expand your influence, which expands the ministry, which ultimately introduces more people to Christ. Leadership development provides the process whereby God may increase ministry without it overwhelming or burning out current leadership.

As with every area in our lives, each step must include God's part and our part. He has already begun the leader-development process in each of our lives, and he asks us to go and do likewise with the leaders he has placed around us. Leaders must constantly and intentionally maintain the balance between trusting God completely (no effort on our part) and focusing solely on completing the task (forgetting to trust God in the process).

Before we discuss the roadmap that Jethro laid out, let me pause and note that this journey is available for everyone. There are no asterisks in this passage that would exclude people affected by disability. It does not matter if somebody uses a wheelchair, has a developmental delay, or is on the autism spectrum. God calls everybody into some level of influence, and we must diligently keep our doors wide open to every person who is called to serve in a position of leadership. Do not allow the fear of the unknown or your flawed human eyes to skip over a potential leader. Prayerfully connect with God, ask for his eyes and perspective, and be willing to journey with everybody God calls you to serve.

MODEL: "You shall represent the people before God and bring their cases to God."

In John 13, we read the story of Jesus washing the feet of his disciples. He acted with humility and grace, willfully placing himself in the role of a servant and preferring his disciples before himself. He had every right to demand that his own feet be washed. He could have preached a sermon on honoring leaders properly. Instead, he modeled the heart of God and set the example that we should serve and care for those we lead. He was the ultimate model of a servant leader.

Before we can consider recruiting, training, and equipping others for leadership, we must be the kind of leader we are looking for. At this point, this is far less about skills and more about character, integrity, and faithfulness. We naturally follow and learn from what we can see and experience. Leadership is full of maxims and they exist because they are true. We know that if nobody is following us, then we are simply going on a walk. It is well known that effective leadership begins within ourselves. Great leadership is knowing what you do not know and then building a team accordingly. You cannot discover and develop what you are not. You cannot take people where you have never been, and you cannot ask of people what you are not willing to do on your own. We must all be willing to walk the steps and live the life that we feel compelled to invite others into. We are all on the same journey; the only difference is that we are in unique places on the journey.

So, what are the key characteristics of effective and healthy leadership? What should we all strive to live and model in our daily life? There are five characteristics that seem to be the earmarks of truly irresistible leaders:

1. *Character*—Perhaps the simplest explanation of this concept is who you are when nobody is looking. It is much easier to live well and do the right thing when the crowd is watching you. But how do you live when you are alone, in the shadows, or even out of town? Do you live with the reality that God never leaves you or forsakes you? Or do you have a double standard for your life where your words, actions, and attitudes might not line up? Healthy character means that you say what you mean, and you mean what you say. It means that when those you lead see you in church or out in the community, you are the same person. It means that you are allowing God to direct your steps regardless of the audience, remembering that at the end of the day you are truly living your life for him.

2. *Passion*—Are you leading in an area that excites you? What do you find keeps you up at night or triggers your emotions when you hear a poignant story? What aspect of your leadership would you do for free or what can you simply not stop talking about? For me, this book is an expression of my passion. I could talk about leadership development all

day; I passionately pursue new leaders and prayerfully help them in the journey God has called them into. Maybe your passion is public speaking, writing, running programs, or planning events. Find your passion and work hard to lead as much as you can from your sweet spot. If you are unsure what your passion is, ask the people in your life to whom you are closest. They will most likely be able to tell you what you always talk about or what draws out your emotions.

3. *Responsibility*—A major hallmark of effective leadership is a sense of personal responsibility. Healthy leaders accept appropriate blame and deflect praise. Do you do all that you can to shine the spotlight on those around you? Or do you find yourself frequently talking about your own accomplishments? Responsibility means owning your mistakes. Regardless of where on the chain of leadership the breakdown occurred, if I am the team leader, then I am responsible for the mistake. When talking about team members publicly, be generous with your praise. If correction or redirection is necessary, that should happen in private. A responsible leader remembers that the relationship with fellow leaders always outweighs the accomplishment of the task.

4. *Compassion*—Godly leadership is about relationships and helping people draw closer to God. Compassion can often be measured by how much time you spend praying for those you lead versus teaching or equipping those you lead. Time after time we see that Jesus was moved by compassion as he looked out over crowds and communities. His heart broke and he wept openly for the city of Jerusalem (see Luke 19:41-44). Do you find yourself leading more from your head than your heart? While your head might have great strategies and ideas, without the heart there is a much smaller chance of having sustainable impact. King Saul tried to figure many things out in his own strength, while David is described as a man after God's own heart. Which legacy do you desire as the description of your leadership?

5. *Generosity*—Do you look for opportunities to bless others with time, money, advice, and praise? Is your desire for leadership ultimately to fill your own selfish wants and needs, or is it to set those around you up for success? While there are times when we must say no to others to maintain healthy personal boundaries, leadership must ultimately be about giving ourselves away for the betterment of those who are following us. A former boss of mine lives by the

personal and professional mantra of being unreasonably generous. We are to bestow the mercy and grace on others that God has so generously poured out into our lives. When an opportunity to give crosses your path, what are your initial emotions and ultimate actions? Be a generous leader in every respect, and I believe that God will bless your leadership far beyond your wildest dreams—ultimately allowing you to better lead and give even more generously.

IDENTIFY: "look for able men from all the people . . . and place such men over the people . . . "

As we seek out potential leaders to raise up, we must prayerfully ask God for help to see others the way that he does. It is easy to follow the example of Samuel, who wanted to anoint David's older brother based upon his appearance. Too often, I find myself focusing on the external qualities of an individual as a determination of leadership potential. Charisma, friendliness, speaking ability, and management skills can become the basis for signing somebody up. Instead, we ought to identify leadership God's way. In Judges 6, we find Gideon hiding in the bottom of a winepress while he threshes wheat in order to keep his grain away from the invading Midianites. This is hardly a picture of strong potential leadership! Yet, the angel of the Lord appears and declares, "Mighty hero, the Lord is with you!" Gideon saw himself as the least valuable member of the weakest clan within his tribe. Yet, God saw so much more. Gideon grew into the leadership role that God had for him and delivered Israel from devastating oppression at the hands of the Midianites.

Remember that God looks at the heart, the character, the spirit of an individual. To identify potential leaders is not a matter of assessing their skills, talents, and abilities. It begins with the acknowledgment of their leadership calling and their character. Only God truly knows this, so intentional prayer and discernment are key at this stage of leadership development.

Our churches are filled with volunteers who serve faithfully throughout the ministry. One challenge of developing leaders is finding the right individuals to develop. What is the difference between a faithful volunteer and a leader? Look for people who already have a following. The informal influencer is living out leadership by making a difference in their volunteer role. This does not need to be limited to the influence you see within your church community. Perhaps you can identify leadership potential in someone who is working as a local store manager, running a non-profit, or serving in some other leadership role within your community. It might be that they have not yet been invited into leadership at church but are simply waiting for that door to open.

Look for individuals who make things happen. They take the direction or guidance given to them and then exponentially expand the task. They see things through to completion regardless of the obstacles. They rally other volunteers around them, they respond well to responsibilities given to them, and one of their most frequent questions is simply, "What's next?"

As you begin to identify potential leaders, I would encourage you to keep your eyes open for two types of people. Seek out the people who (1) fill your leadership gaps, and (2) will replace you. Nobody will remain in a leadership role forever. Effective leaders serve like they will finish their race in their current role while leading with the sensibility that they might be called to leave tomorrow. My goal in every place of ministry where I lead is to build a team that will do things better than I can alone and will last longer than my time there.

Who fills in your gaps? Each of us has certain skills and talents where we would score a 10 on a scale of 1 to 10. Identify the places where you are a 10 and then ask God to bring you the individuals who are a 10 in the areas where you are weak. This creates a well-rounded team that holistically fulfills all the basic needs of leadership. Strategic planning, administrative support, public speaking, team building, and so many other areas of leadership exist. No one person will ever be the ultimate leader in every aspect of leadership. God designed us to work together as a team, not to lead from a place of isolation. In addition, identifying others who fill your gaps allows for different personalities, perspectives, and experiences to all come together to form a dynamic leadership group that will lead and serve people well.

Who will replace you? In the process of identifying leaders to help fill your own gaps, you will undoubtedly discover people who are a 10 in the same areas that you are. When this happens, you might be tempted to close the door to them as potential leaders out of fear, insecurity, or pride. A better option would be to prayerfully consider your succession plan. Elijah had Elisha, David had Solomon, and Jesus had his disciples. As you lead, it is wise to prayerfully place your next steps firmly in God's hands with the sensibility that you are stewarding his ministry in all things.

Another important aspect of identification is to seek out leaders, not followers. While every leader must be a follower, not every follower is called to lead. Three basic characteristics will help you identify potential leaders. First, leaders have initiative—look for people who are stepping out and failing forward. As you observe the people under your leadership, watch their actions and attitudes, paying special attention to those who are willing to take risks. Leaders generally enjoy trying something new, they will often move forward without all the answers, and they are willing to fail in order to learn and grow. Second, leaders are also typically innovative—identify those who tend to see things differently. True leaders do not simply conform to the status quo, but they are consistently looking for better and more efficient methods of operation. When somebody approaches you with a crazy idea that nobody has ever considered, much less tried, it might be a sign that you have a leader ready for development. Finally, leaders have influence—carefully notice the atmosphere of the room when people come and go. This has nothing to do with title or responsibilities. Rather, it is about the informal influence people have and how others respond to their words, attitudes, and actions. Seek out the individuals to whom others turn for assistance, lean on for support, or rally around during times of change or growth. Influence is a powerful component of leadership that can rarely be taught but is essential to have.

COACH: " . . . make them know the way in which must walk and what they must do."

We first meet Joshua in the pages of the Bible as a military general who goes out to battle against the Amalekites under the direction of Moses. It is said that, "Moses commanded Joshua, and so Joshua did" (Joshua 11:15), ultimately leading to a resounding victory for the Israelites. The relationship between Moses and Joshua continued to grow so that Joshua was later considered to be the apprentice of Moses, and he was allowed to approach God's mountain alongside Moses. Joshua was with Moses as he dealt with the rebellion concerning the golden calf. Joshua was granted permission to enter the Tent of Meeting that was typically reserved for the face-to-face conversations between God and Moses. He was one of the twelve spies and one of the only two who believed God for victory in Canaan. Deuteronomy 31:7 reveals the pinnacle of this coaching relationship as Moses declared to Joshua in the presence of all Israel, "Be strong and courageous, for you shall go with this people into the land that the Lord has sworn to their fathers to give them and you shall put them in possession of it." Shortly after this, God personally commissioned Joshua as the new leader of Israel.

How did this come about? Moses was a model of godly leadership, and he identified Joshua as a potential leader. Then, a coaching relationship began that lasted decades. God used Moses to develop Joshua into the leader that God was calling him to be. What does a healthy coaching relationship look like? The following four principles will allow you to coach potential leaders so that when God calls, they are ready to lead without you:

1. The first step is to believe in them as potential leaders. This is not merely by words but is more accurately expressed through actions. I try to show someone that I believe in their leadership skills by giving them areas of responsibility in which to lead. Moses saw Joshua's potential and put him in charge of the fighting forces in the desert early in their friendship. As leaders,

we must be willing to pull back on our involvement, allowing others to reveal their own leadership skills.

2. The next principle of a healthy coaching relationship is to always consider them as a person not as a tool. If I am looking to a person simply to complete a task and I only train them at a skill level, I miss the entire aspect of their personhood. Leadership is about character, integrity, and people skills, along with practical talent and ability. Coaching is a holistic approach that speaks into every aspect of leadership from the heart to the hands to the daily habits.

3. Next, we should respond to the immediate needs in our day-to-day environment while always maintaining a focus on the bigger picture. A healthy coaching relationship keeps the end goal in mind while performing daily functions. If we allow busyness to dictate our coaching, we may end up teaching skills that only have temporary application. This would shortchange the potential of the coaching relationship and hinder effective leadership development in those around us.

4. The final principle of coaching is the ability to guide others to places of transformation; set them up for a series of aha moments! While I can teach, mentor, model, and coach all day long, nothing compares to the moment when an individual truly gets it. This involves their emotions, their confidence, their competence, and their excitement. When somebody discovers that they have mastered a skill or determined a course of action, it has the potential to transform and expand the capacity of their leadership. Liken this to a child learning to ride a bike. When the training wheels are taken off, it is scary at first. But all it takes is one ride with proper balance before the child begins attempting greater speeds, learning to jump, and pushing the limits of their bicycle. Without the aha moments, leadership will remain stunted and confined to training wheels.

RELEASE: "and let them judge the people at all times."

If there has ever been a less likely candidate for ministry leadership than Paul, I cannot think of one. A former church persecutor who dragged Christians to jail simply for their faith was called by God to become one of the most influential leaders in the history of the Church. His story reminds me that an individual's past does not disqualify them from leadership. Often, it is the very brokenness from our past and God's gracious redemption that create the ideal leader. In Acts 13, we see the final component of leadership development displayed in the life of Paul. At the urging of the Holy Spirt, Paul (along with Barnabas) is appointed as a leader and released to go and walk freely in the calling God placed upon his life.

One of the most challenging aspects of developing leaders is the ability to truly release them. So many questions might arise: *Are they ready? Did I equip them well? What if they are better than me? What if they fail?* The truth is, all these questions are far too focused on myself and they clearly discredit God's work. There must come a time when developing leaders are free to walk in the calling and training they have received. Will it look different from how you envisioned it? Probably. Will their leadership style blaze new trails? Hopefully. Will we be blessed to say that we had a small part in the ministry they now lead? Absolutely—this is a wonderful benefit of developing leaders. When I move toward releasing a leader into ministry, I follow the four steps listed below:

1. Throughout this journey of leadership, it is imperative that we provide appropriate tasks over which leaders can take ownership. Start small, and as they continue to grow, increase the size or scope of the task while providing less hands-on support. Developing leaders must learn where their skill and maturity are lacking and where they are growing so that they can adapt accordingly. It will be very difficult for this to happen if they do not have the opportunity to lead an endeavor on their own, regardless of size or complexity.

2. Another important step to releasing leaders is to not only allow for different methods, but to also intentionally encourage leaders to try their own ideas or perspectives. As there are many great ways to tackle a project, it is typically less about which route you choose and more about the completion itself.

3. As growing leaders step out into new and uncomfortable scenarios, they will inevitably miss the mark and fail on a project. Effective leaders should celebrate failure as a launching pad for growth. How else can we grow unless we learn what does not work? In my life, time and time again, failing forward has been the best learning

opportunity. It humbles me, forces me to re-evaluate, makes me listen to others, and puts me back on my knees in prayer. If every task and project was successful on the first attempt, my tendency would be to lean on my own understanding and forget that I need God and others to succeed. In terms of leadership development, I prefer somebody who will take risks that could possibly end in failure instead of somebody I need to compel into action. This goes back to one of our previously established leadership characteristics of initiative.

4. Finally, you must remain available as needed. This follows the frequently used mentoring model of "I do; you watch. I do; you help. You do; I help. You do; I watch." Even as new leaders begin to venture out on their own, we must always be willing to provide input, advice, and clarity for whatever leadership challenges they might face. While the relationship needs are determined by them, we would provide a disservice if we closed the door to future relationship with them. This is another great reminder to see potential leaders as people instead of as tools to accomplish a task.

One side benefit of developing leaders is that you will gain accountability. If you are leading from a place of isolation, there is a tendency to become lazy, to cut corners, and to focus merely on task completion. Surrounding yourself with hungry and excited leaders keeps your own leadership skills sharp and relevant. Sustainable leaders remain both learners and teachers throughout their leadership journey, which, in turn, allows God to entrust them with more leadership opportunities. I encourage you to stay humble and vulnerable through the process. As you work to develop emerging leaders, keep in mind that it is OK that you will not have all the answers that they have a unique God-given perspective to share, and that the journey is just as important as the destination.

Leadership Considerations for People Affected by Disability

A crucial element of irresistible leadership is to ensure that the roadmap to leadership is open for everybody who feels called. We simply cannot allow disabilities to hinder the development of leadership in the kingdom of God. However, there are certain considerations we should be aware of as we work to create a successful roadmap for those following us.

A professional mentoring relationship already proves to be one of the harder relationships to manage. It requires a certain level of intimacy to understand and develop personal skillsets. But it also must have boundaries to maintain a chain of command. The challenges of providing leadership development for someone with a disability are considerably more complex because of the sensitivity of their life experiences. However, these same experiences can often prove to be just as beneficial.

Approaching an individual affected by disability with the offer of any kind of relationship, whether it is friendship, mentorship, or of a professional nature, requires some forethought. Your relationship will probably not be a casual one. Therefore, you must be prepared for what their expectations might be. Quite often, your friend affected by disability will not have the varying types of relationships that typical people do because their disability may have limited their social interaction. Therefore, they might never have received the opportunity to learn how to navigate varying types and degrees of relationships. Often, they tend to view every relationship through a close, intimate filter. The benefit of this is that they will probably be some of your most eager leaders. They generally follow instruction to the best of their ability and work hard to improve.

As you begin to work with individuals affected by disability within a leadership context, you should be aware of the unique dynamics involved as it will help you form your leadership-development strategy. In the same way that each person is unique, the following points are general and may not be true for everyone.

- People affected by disability typically filter their life experiences and relationships differently because of their limitations and their unique skill sets.
- They are generally eager to do or try any task you might ask of them.
- People affected by disability tend to live in extremes. Either they have been sheltered from many life experiences and are not ready to enter the world on their own, or they may have been traumatized through abuse or neglect, or they may even have been placed in situations where they were expected to function in a way that they are simply unable to.

- There may be a lack of community with their peers. People affected by disability often only engage in family relationships or befriend people older than them who are more open to accepting them for who they are.
- Be prepared for the potential of limited social skills due to their inability to have relationships with their peers. A part of their leadership roadmap should include opportunities to develop peer friendships.
- They can have compulsive behavior that stems from the need to feel independent. It might take more patience on your part and greater intentionality when teaching leadership concepts.
- Our friends affected by disability often lack confidence in their natural abilities and might struggle with viewing their disability as purely negative. They may need assistance in seeing and understanding the positives that can come from how God uniquely made them.

Here are some tips to consider when creating a successful leadership-development relationship with individuals affected by disability:

- Understand that the relationship you form with them is personal for them, not just professional. You may be the first person who has ever shown interest in developing them and their skills. This will often result in a very strong bond from their perspective.
- Try to introduce them to a group of peers who will genuinely embrace them. You want to protect both yourself and your friend from an unhealthy attachment if you are one of the few, if not the only person, showing interest in their well-being.
- Understand that they may require much closer guidance and instruction than a typical emerging leader. Because of this, you should endeavor to provide instruction in a variety of ways.
- They may not pick up on social cues or subtle hints. Clear, direct communication is always best.
- Do not lower your standards if they don't reach a goal on their first attempt. First, try a different approach or be more involved by providing a step-by-step process. They are probably used to people lowering standards just because they have a disability. This is generally more patronizing than helpful. If anything, lowering standards encourages a false sense of accomplishment, and it

will only hurt them when they realize how ill-equipped they are to navigate the real world.

- Help them see their disability in a positive light. There will probably always be hindrances because of their disability, but helping them find the "perks" of having a disability can provide them with confidence and valuable perspective.
- Praise the little victories as much as possible. Remember that the journey is just as valuable as the destination. Every opportunity for praise and encouragement makes a difference.

As you walk the leadership-development journey with friends affected by disability, be patient, be gracious, and be understanding. Establish boundaries and uphold expectations, but never forget that God has created each of us uniquely and that leadership comes in many different forms.

When the Roadmap Does Not Work

Contrary to what we all hope for, there are times when the roadmap for leadership development breaks down. Perhaps it is the process itself or the opportunities presented. Maybe the individual in training learns that they are not truly called to leadership or they do not have the capacity to continue. At times, it might even be because of our own shortcomings as a leader. Regardless of the reason, we must lead well when this happens to maintain relationship and continue the healthy culture of irresistible leadership that we have worked so hard to create. Let's take a closer look at the ways the leadership-development roadmap may break down.

The Leader—Whenever there is a breakdown in the roadmap to leadership, it is essential that we look to ourselves first as the potential issue. *Are my expectations unrealistic for the individual that I am developing? Have I been clear and concise in communicating the expectations and the process to them?* Perhaps I might discover that I am micro-managing my team and hindering their ability to truly grow and develop as leaders. A self-assessment is essential before determining any course of action. At this point in the process, you may also consider seeking feedback from other leaders around you. Self-awareness is always enhanced by the vulnerability of listening to others.

- My time—how much time am I truly investing into the leadership relationship?

- My energy—are the people I am leading getting my best energy or my leftovers?
- My character—am I living out the expectations I am placing on others?
- My vision—am I pressing people into my vision or have I submitted my vision to God?
- My capacity—am I attempting to develop too many leaders or handle too many tasks? Do I need to step back, trim down my to-do list, and focus well on a few items instead of poorly handling many items?

The Process—If I truly believe that I am in a good place as a leader, that the vision is clear and concise, and that expectations are attainable, then it is time to look at the process. The tendency of leaders is to continually add to a plan or system without removing items that are no longer valid. A long, hard look at the process might reveal too many steps to advancement, too many tasks to accomplish, or too many resources to digest. Any one of these areas might overwhelm your team to the point where they can no longer grow and develop as leaders.

- Steps to take—ideally, each task or project should have three basic steps to follow. If you find that your projects have more than that, it might be time to simplify them into smaller, more manageable steps.

- Tasks to accomplish—often, we find ourselves as leaders saying yes to every good opportunity that comes along, instead of waiting for the best opportunities. Great leaders know what matters, they stay on course, and they are not afraid to say no to anything that will pull them away from their passion and calling. This is not to say that seasons will not arise where you are assisting outside of your sweet spot. That is part of servant leadership. However, if your task list seems to be more about the projects of others and less about your own, then it is probably time for a redirect.

- Resources to digest—I must confess that I have a book addiction. I buy books faster than I can read them, both at work and at home. While this works for me, it can be devastating to those who are following me if I place an unrealistic expectation on them regarding reading and digesting resources. The ideal ratio is to share one resource with your team out of every ten books or resources with which you engage. In addition, provide a feedback loop to ensure that the resource becomes significant and is not merely busy work that distracts your team from their tasks.

The Recipient—When you can determine that your personal leadership is healthy and that the process is viable, then it might become necessary to assess the individual you are coaching to determine if they are truly in the right place. This does not necessarily invalidate their calling to leadership; it merely causes you to assess whether this is the ideal time and opportunity for them to develop their leadership skills.

- Time—is this individual being pushed to move faster than their capacity allows, placing them in a situation that they are unable to navigate? Addressing this might feel awkward and painful, but these conversations can be invaluable as they actually steer us back to where we truly need to be.
- Role—if somebody feels called to public speaking and teaching, but we place them in an

administrative support role, it is only a matter of time before the process begins to break down. Regular check-ups with your team will help you to assess if they are still in a role that best suits their calling.

- Personal—has something happened to them on a personal level that is causing the decline in leadership development? Perhaps there is an illness with a family member, or a financial difficulty, or even a moral failure. A personal setback does not have to be a permanent removal from leadership development, but it might signal the need to pause the process until strengthening, stability, or restoration may take place.

Results of Leadership

We have considered the reality of leadership. It is personal, it is a calling, and it involves self-awareness in terms of your relationship with God and your relationship with others. An irresistible leader goes even further and looks intently at the abilities of others and does not allow disability to disqualify any potential leader. The roadmap of leadership development is a process of modeling, identifying, coaching and releasing others into the leadership roles and responsibility that God has called them to. So, where does all this lead? What are the results of effective and irresistible leadership? As stated earlier, the ultimate result is bringing glory to God. If we do everything with a heart to honor him, and we are faithful to the calling on our lives by inviting others to join us on the journey of leadership, then I have full confidence that our churches and ministries will be shining beacons of God's glory. Along with this, there are several other general results of leadership that will bless you and your ministry moving forward.

Influence and sustainability

Leadership provides a platform to expand influence and create sustainability. A major question that faces every church and ministry is, what will happen when their leader leaves? Regardless of the reason, every leader will eventually give up their role, and the organization will find itself in crisis unless effective leadership principles are in place. The roadmap of leadership development will result in increased influence. By intentionally seeking others to engage in the journey, you will expand the number of people with whom you interact. Then, as these leaders begin to grow through your coaching, your influence will expand exponentially as every leader that you have touched begins to influence countless other individuals. While it may be impossible to truly calculate influence, we can still get a pretty good general idea. I remember working for a pizza company in college. They taught us that every customer would talk to ten other people about the quality of our service and product. Using that as a baseline, consider the size of your team, your ministry, or your church, and multiply that number by ten. This is a very conservative estimate of the scope of influence that your leadership might have.

In addition to influence, effective leadership provides sustainability. There is a pipeline of new leaders ready to step in when one leader is no longer able to fulfill their role, allowing the ministry to continue and even expand. Because of leadership, relationships are sustained, vision is sustained, and health within the organization is sustained. Sustainability only happens when leaders spend more energy communicating the vision and empowering other leaders than focusing on themselves. A self-focused leader is simply incapable of providing a sustainable model. Throughout the Bible, there are countless examples of God's truth being faithfully passed from one leader to another. The vision never changes, but the personality of the leader and the methodology of execution vary widely. Sustainability allows for personal differences and preferences without sacrificing the plans and calling of God. Irresistible leaders are constantly aware that ministry is larger than they are; they prayerfully and intentionally lead with this sensibility.

Helping others succeed

The final command of Jesus involves believers going out and making disciples of all nations. Discipleship is not solely about salvation. Rather, it is about teaching people how to live the life for which God created them. Leadership is a part of this journey for some individuals. A natural result of irresistible leadership is for your sphere of influence to be a place where people are working more toward helping others succeed than worrying about their own success. One of my colleagues talks about her basic philosophy of life as striving for obscurity. If God wants to promote, to spotlight, or to in any other way expand her influence, then he is more than capable of accomplishing that. Her focus is on serving and leading others well. This is such a different sensibility from the world's idea of stepping on others in order to get ahead. Imagine the true joy you would experience every day as you see people whom you have the privilege of coaching find success. Imagine the satisfaction when somebody whom you identified as a leader has influence far beyond your own scope. Preferring others above ourselves is foundational to how Jesus established the church, and our leadership must reflect this attitude of servanthood.

Advocacy

A final result of irresistible leadership is the ability to stand in the gap for young leaders, new leaders, and leaders affected by disability, thereby allowing them the opportunity to lead. By resisting autocratic and domineering leadership, we are able to make space for every member of the body of Christ to serve and lead according to their gifts and calling. Advocacy is simply speaking on behalf of or in support of another person. While you and I understand the reality that a disability does not diminish the leadership capacity of an individual, not every leader within the church does. *Are You Ready?*, another book in the *Irresistible Church* series, provides the biblical foundation and perspective regarding disability ministry that you might be looking for as you step into the role of advocate. Advocacy engages in difficult conversations; advocacy speaks on behalf of others; advocacy defends and fights to advance the concept of allowing everybody to fully belong. You have the ability to shine a spotlight on the leadership capabilities of your friends affected by disability in such a way that others are compelled to see and can no longer dismiss a valuable member of God's leadership plan.

There are times when disability requires reasonable accommodations in order for influence to expand. Whether it is a wheelchair or a communication device or helping others slow down to engage in conversation, these accommodations are a minimal ask on the part of leaders when compared to the tremendous blessings and transformational culture experienced as leadership doors are opened wide. Do not let accommodations or other perceived hindrances slow down the roadmap to leadership development. Continue to stand firm, invite all who are called into the journey, and watch God bless your advocacy efforts.

Final Thoughts

Ultimately, leadership development is less about you and more about others. It involves daily setting aside your rights and asking God for the next steps to take with each person whom you influence. It is about making space for everybody in the body of Christ to serve and lead, understanding that calling is a much stronger reason to engage in leadership than a disability could ever be a hindrance to avoid leadership. Thank you for being an irresistible leader! Thank you for doing your part to help your church or ministry open its doors a bit wider so that people of all abilities may fully belong. Be encouraged that you are not alone, that you are right where God wants you to be, and that the scope and impact of your leadership are far beyond anything you could ever hope or imagine. Thank you, and please keep fighting the good fight, inviting as many people as you can into the wonderful journey of leadership development.

Becoming *Irresistible*

Luke 14 commands Christ followers to "Go quickly . . . find the blind, the lame, and the crippled . . . and compel them to come in!" While this sounds inspiring and daunting, exciting and overwhelming, motivating and frightening, all at the same time, what does it actually mean? How do we live and function within the church in such a way that families affected by disability are compelled to walk through our doors to experience the body of Christ?

We can certainly *compel* them by offering programs, ministries, events, and other church activities, but what if the compelling aspect was more about heart, culture, acceptance and embracing? What if our churches were overflowing with the hope of Jesus Christ . . . a hope not simply for those who "fit in" or look the part, but rather a hope to all, including the marginalized, downtrodden and outcast?

Becoming *Irresistible* is more than programs and activities—it is about a transformational work in our hearts . . . first as individuals and then as the body of Christ. *Irresistible* allows us to see each individual as he or she truly is: created in the image of God (Genesis 1:26-27), designed purposely as a masterpiece (Psalm 139:13-14), instilled with purpose, plans and dreams (Jeremiah 29:11), and a truly indispensable member of the kingdom of God (1 Corinthians 12:23). An *Irresistible Church* is an "authentic community built on the hope of Christ that compels people affected by disability to fully belong." It is powerful for a person to know that he or she is fully welcomed and belongs. *Irresistible* captures the heart of the church as it should be—how else do we explain the rapid growth and intense attraction to the church in the book of Acts? The heart of God was embodied through the people of God by the Spirit of God . . . and that is simply *Irresistible*!

The Irresistible Church Series is designed to help not only shape and transform the heart of the church, but also to provide the practical steps and activities to put *flesh* around the *heart* of the church—to help your church become a place for people to fully belong. Thank you for responding to the call to become *Irresistible*. It will not happen overnight, but it will happen. As with all good things, it requires patience and perseverance, determination and dedication, and ultimately an underlying trust in the faithfulness of God. May God bless you on this journey. Be assured that you are not alone—there are many on the path of *Irresistible*.

For more information or to join the community,
please visit www.irresistiblechurch.org.

Joni and Friends
INTERNATIONAL DISABILITY CENTER

Joni and Friends was established in 1979 by Joni Eareckson Tada, who at 17 was injured in a diving accident, leaving her a quadriplegic. Since its inception, Joni and Friends has been dedicated to extending the love and message of Christ to people who are affected by disability whether it is the disabled person, a family member, or friend. Our objective is to meet the physical, emotional, and spiritual needs of this group of people in practical ways.

Joni and Friends is committed to recruiting, training, and motivating new generations of people with disabilities to become leaders in their churches and communities. Today, the Joni and Friends International Disability Center serves as the administrative hub for an array of programs which provide outreach to thousands of families affected by disability around the globe. These include two radio programs, an award-winning television series, the Wheels for the World international wheelchair distribution ministry, Family Retreats which provide respite for those with disabilities and their families, Field Services to provide church training along with educational and inspirational resources at a local level, and the Christian Institute on Disability to establish a firm biblical worldview on disability-related issues.

From local neighborhoods to the far reaches of the world, Joni and Friends is striving to demonstrate to people affected by disability, in tangible ways, that God has not abandoned them—he is with them—providing love, hope, and eternal salvation.

Available Now in the Irresistible Church Series

Start with Hello
Introducing Your Church to Special Needs Ministry

Families with special needs often share that they desire two things in their church: accessibility and acceptance. Accessibility to existing structures, programs and people is an imperative. Acceptance with a sense of belonging by the others who also participate in the structures, programs and fellowship of the church is equally necessary. In this simple book you'll learn the five steps to becoming an accessible and accepting church.

To receive first notice of upcoming resources, including respite, inclusive worship and support groups, please contact us at churchrelations@joniandfriends.org.

Available Now in the Irresistible Church Series

We've Got This!
Providing Respite for Families Affected by Disability

Families or caregivers who have children with disabilities are often isolated, exhausted, and grieving. Respite events can be a safe bridge for families to cross over the threshold of the church by satisfying an urgent need. A place for children to be themselves, for caregivers to have a break and for the church to serve well is invaluable. This book is a practical guide that provides the necessary tools to plan and execute a successful respite event.

To receive first notice of upcoming resources, including respite, inclusive worship and support groups, please contact us at churchrelations@joniandfriends.org.

Available Now in the Irresistible Church Series

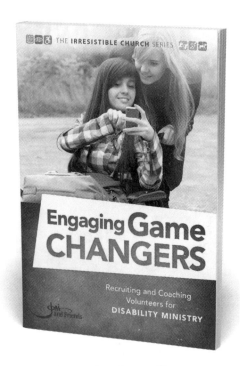

Engaging Game Changers
Recruiting and Coaching Volunteers for Disability Ministry

The breadth of impact any ministry has for the individuals they serve is dependent on the volunteers who are recruited to be the hands and feet of Jesus. This resource will train you as a ministry leader to identify and recruit, thoroughly train, then release volunteers who will serve families affected by special needs effectively and with the love of Christ.

To receive first notice of upcoming resources, including respite, inclusive worship and support groups, please contact us at churchrelations@joniandfriends.org.

Available Now in the Irresistible Church Series

Are You Ready
A Personal Guide to Disability Ministry for the Reluctant Leader

Does the thought of engaging in disability ministry make you nervous? Are you unclear on how to lead others as you serve and embrace individuals affected by disability? As you read the pages of this book, you will learn the biblical perspective regarding disability, consider both the heart of a leader and the heart of the church, and begin to recognize and serve your community's practical needs. Together, you and your team will see the development and growth of a truly Irresistible Church.

To receive first notice of upcoming resources, including respite, inclusive worship and support groups, please contact us at churchrelations@joniandfriends.org.

Available Now in the Irresistible Church Series

Call Me Friend
Building Compelling Relationships Through One-on-One Ministry

For the ministry leader who desires to include people of all ages with special needs in the life of the church, this practical guide to buddy ministry provides clear, concise direction on how to organize and implement this effective ministry model. Leaders will discover how buddies provide discipleship, friendship, safety, participation, communication and positive behavior management. The simple steps you'll find in this book will build relationships and assist your church in becoming an authentic community where all people may fully belong.

To receive first notice of upcoming resources, including respite, inclusive worship and support groups, please contact us at churchrelations@joniandfriends.org.

Available Now in the Irresistible Church Series

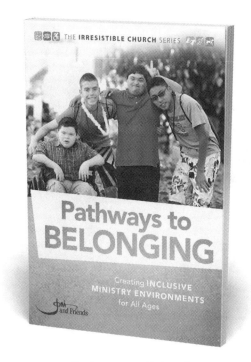

Pathways to Belonging
Creating Inclusive Ministry Environments for All Ages

Church leaders with a heart to serve families affected by disability frequently ask, "How do I know the best way to include each special friend when their needs vary?" This book is a response to that question, offering step-by-step tools for evaluating the needs of friends with disabilities and creating a culture that welcomes these individuals and their families. Within these pages, we discuss creating accessible environments that provide access to the gospel while being sensitive to learning styles and physical needs.

To receive first notice of upcoming resources, including respite, inclusive worship and support groups, please contact us at churchrelations@joniandfriends.org.

Available Now in the Irresistible Church Series

Shout for JOY!
Engaging the Whole Church in Accessible Worship

Do you long to be part of a church community where people of all abilities gather to worship, a church where the sounds of worship include a wheelchair rolling down the aisle, the tap of a cane, and the sound of people with differing intellectual disabilities lifting their voices together in praise and prayer? If so, we pray that *Shout for Joy!* will help your church have a heart for worship that is accessible to all and give you some practical "how-to" ideas as well.

To receive first notice of upcoming resources, including respite, inclusive worship and support groups, please contact us at churchrelations@joniandfriends.org.

Other Recommended Resources

Beyond Suffering Bible	***Beyond Suffering® Student Edition***	***Joni: An Unforgettable Story***

The *Beyond Suffering Bible* by Joni and Friends is the first study Bible made specifically for those who suffer and the people who love them. Uplifting insights from Joni Eareckson Tada and numerous experts and scholars who have experienced suffering in their own lives and will help you move beyond the "why" of suffering to grasp the eternal value God is building into our lives. Special features include: inspiring devotionals, biblical and contemporary profiles, Bible reading plans, connection points and disability ministry resources.

Beyond Suffering for the Next Generation: A Christian View on Disability Ministry will equip young people to consider the issues that affect people with disabilities and their families, and inspire them to action. Students who embrace this study will gain confidence to join a growing, worldwide movement that God is orchestrating to fulfill Luke 14:21-23: "Go out quickly into the streets and alleys of the town and bring in the poor, the crippled, the blind, and the lame.... so that my house will be full."

In this unforgettable autobiography, Joni reveals each step of her struggle to accept her disability and discover the meaning of her life. The hard-earned truths she discovers and the special ways God reveals his love are testimonies to faith's triumph over hardship and suffering. This new edition includes an afterword, in which Joni talks about the events that have occurred in her life since the book's original publication in 1976, including her marriage and the expansion of her worldwide ministry to families affected by disability.

Find out more at http://
www.joniandfriends.org/
store/category/bibles/

ISBN: 978-0-9838484-6-2
304 pages · 8.5" x 11"
Includes CD-ROM

ISBN: 978-0310240013
205 pages · Paperback

www.joniandfriends.org · P.O. Box 3333, Agoura Hills, CA 91376
(818) 707-5664 · Fax: (818) 707-2391 TTY: (818) 707-9707

Customizable Resources from the Book

Available for Download at
http://www.irresistiblechurch.org/library

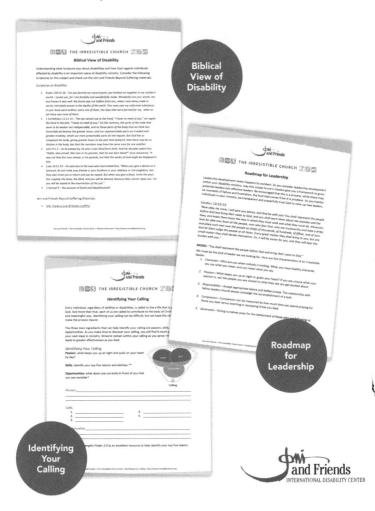